Dyla

For
Ann and Megan

First Impression—1999
Second Impression—2003
Third Impression—2006

ISBN 1 85902 629 X
ISBN-13 9781859026298

© David Rowe
© Extracts from the writings of Dylan Thomas: Dylan Thomas estate.

David Rowe has asserted his right under the Copyright, Designs and
Patents Act, 1988, to be identified as Author of this Work.

All rights reserved. No part of this book may be reproduced, stored in a
retrieval system, or transmitted in any form or by any means, electronic,
electrostatic, magnetic tape, mechanical, photocopying, recording or
otherwise without permission in writing from the publishers,
Gomer Press, Llandysul, Ceredigion, Wales.

Designed by Olwen Fowler.

Printed in Wales at
Gomer Press, Llandysul, Ceredigion, Wales.

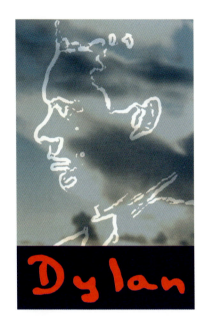

Fern Hill
to Milk Wood

David Rowe

Gomer

foam   walled   crew   brain
ghost   scrawled   do   save
flown   crawled   shoot   day
stone   shawled   grout   fail
toll   clawed   move   fame
blow   stored   groove   wave
growth   shored   brood   grave
abode   floored   mood   pave
bone   forth torn   food   rave
boat   torch worn   loose   slave
code   for   roof   bray
coal   or   proof   array
comb bail   moor   soothe   slay
coma coat   more   bloom   slay
coat loaf   born   loom   pay
cove home   unborn   truce   grey
folk host   intrude   hay
      hope ball   plume   may
      host squal   gloom   say
      hoe   caught   soon   play
      moss drawn   sway
glad gash   gorge   moon through stag
back mole   horde   choose   rage
black moan   haul   fruit screws
crack note   saw   loom   spade
track nose   lord   space
sack pole   law   babe hail mare   skate
stag robe   paw   safe jail nail   scale
      robe   saga came pace rake stair
cram rogue pork   dale lay pain rail escape
crag roll   raw   face laid pale   slave
      roam sword node lake pave   slave
trap rove   gate lane quail
mass soul   cull again jane race
map   so   scald gape late raid
mad   toll   broad gote made trace
lock road   storm haste make
log   stake sore hate male
lag   stole core   come
pack store war   kneel duck
pad   stove horn leap dove
papped shool gnaw deep dumb
ran   snow   adore beat gull
ram   alas   stall weave luck
sag   wharve reach rub
hack   salt   leech rough
crack   implore teeth suck
grand   before   skull
jab   poor   blood
             taut   pluck
r, pr, tr, cr, haunk   flood
r, dr, gr,   horse   stuck
, pl, cl, fl,   shut
, st, sh,   cause   struck
, th, wh,   course   chuck
str.   buck
                          bud
                          budge
                          hunt

contents

	Introduction	7
Chapter One :	Parables of sunlight	11
Chapter Two :	Poison or grapes	29
Chapter Three :	Fathered and found	55
Conclusion :	Fields of praise	76
	Acknowledgements	79
	Bibliography	80

fern hill

Now as I was young and easy under the apple boughs
About the lilting house and happy as the grass was green,
The night above the dingle starry,
Time let me hail and climb
Golden in the heydays of his eyes,
And honoured among wagons I was prince of the apple towns
And once below a time I lordly had the trees and leaves
Trail with daisies and barley
Down the rivers of the windfall light.

introduction

It is sometimes difficult, even impossible, to establish what is true and what is not true about Dylan Thomas. Friends, critics, colleagues and biographers – many of whom knew him personally, often for many years – disagree on many points. Even his mother swore he was born in 1915, not 1914!

As a man, Dylan Thomas was described as 'exciting', 'stimulating' and 'compelling', a man whose company was so exhilarating that many did not care what price they paid for that company. Others, including his own wife, were, at times, decidedly less enthusiastic.

There is less disagreement about Dylan as an artist, for even stern judges of the man agree that he is an outstanding poet, and he is held in esteem by many of the most eminent people of the twentieth century. In his lifetime he was described as the 'greatest living poet in the English language', as 'nothing short of magnificent'. His poetry has also been described as 'psycho-pathological nonsense', but such comments are rare.

Beyond whatever he was or was not, there are the various images of Dylan to complicate the question even further. Some of these images were created by others for their own ends, such as that of the outrageous, drunken lecher that the media were (and are) so greedy for, or that of the wild Welsh boy who roared through a very brief life. There are also images that Dylan created for himself: in his more buoyant moods, he played the role of the romantic poet doomed to a tragic fate who bestowed his genius upon the world as he heroically laughed in death's face. At less expansive times, he pretended to be the sensitive, penniless, misunderstood artist persecuted by a philistine world.

Fact? Fiction? Legend? Lie? In the end, nobody, not even Dylan, knew who the 'real' Dylan was.

The different pieces of his life are like the fragments of coloured glass in a kaleidoscope: some are of brilliant, sparkling colours; others are rather sombre, even murky. Dylan sheltered a host of contradictory impulses and moods that could take him from deplorable coarseness to the most sublime poetry – and back again. Within moments. Each time you shake the fragments of his life they settle in different patterns, now with the brightest, most joyful elements blinding us with their brilliance: at other times more restrained, threatening colours overwhelm the whole.

This book tries to bring together the various pieces that make up the whole. The reader must decide what pattern they form.

It seems beyond doubt that Dylan Thomas was a man with many and extraordinary virtues – and with some almost equally extraordinary vices. It is beyond doubt that he was an artist whose work has brought pleasure, satisfaction and understanding to millions, and will continue to do so as long as man is interested in the truth about life, in life itself.

The UK Year of Literature and Writing 1995,
held in Swansea, celebrated the work of Dylan Thomas.

CHAPTER ONE

Childhood and

Youth in Paradise

Swansea and Fern Hill

1914 – 1932

Parables of sunlight

Dylan Marlais Thomas was born at 5 Cwmdonkin Drive, Swansea on October 27th, 1914, the second child of David John Thomas, a local school teacher, and of Florence Hannah Thomas, née Williams, housewife.

We are so accustomed to such bald statements of fact that we hardly stop to pay attention: after all, we are all born of two parents, in a certain place, and at a certain time. We use these facts to define our identity – for passport applications, for National Insurance numbers, for appearances in court – but not our individuality.

Yet if we are to start piecing together the life of Dylan Thomas, it is with such facts that we must start, for the man he became was influenced by his family, by a place and a time, and also by his names.

To begin at the beginning:
Dylan as a young child.

I

Dylan is a name from ancient Welsh myth and religion, from the days before the dawn of Christianity, from a thousand years before the English appeared in Britain. Dylan is the son of Arianrhod: she and her son are those half-human, half-divine figures preserved in the tales of *The Mabinogion*.

Marlais is a tribute to one of Dylan's great uncles, and to the values he represented. William Thomas was an archetypal Welsh figure: a cobbler turned preacher, a teacher, a political radical who fought for social justice and reform, a leader of the community – and, of course, a poet, who wrote under the name of Marles. William had taken his adopted, bardic name, as is often done in Wales, from the land in which he lived and to which he was so inextricably linked, for Marlais is the name of the stream that runs through his home village of Brechfa. Dylan himself continued this tradition when he gave the name of a river to his daughter, Aeron.

Dylan's father carried the almost inevitable label of Anglicized Welshmen, David John, and his mother had an English name, but they gave their son names that asserted both their heritage and their hopes, names that evoked both the mysterious prehistory of the Welsh and the values, the language and the culture of modern Wales. The new-born son was tied to both the history and the future of his people.

While the names call up a past that had been lived in the Welsh language, the date and place of his birth did not augur well for a Welsh-language future, for the world of the Welsh was coming under increasing threat.

Swansea was the epitome of a city that comfortably and unself-consciously straddled several worlds: English and Welsh were spoken almost equally when Dylan was born, and there was an important hinterland where Welsh predominated. The city was

math the son of mathonwy

And they brought her unto him, and the maiden came in. 'Damsel,' said he, 'art thou the maiden?' 'I know not, Lord, other than that I am.' Then he took his magic wand, and bent it. 'Step over this,' said he, 'and I shall know if thou art the maiden.' Then she stepped over the magic wand, and there appeared forthwith a fine chubby yellow-haired boy. [...]

'Verily,' said Math the son of Mathonwy, concerning the fine yellow-haired boy, 'I will cause this one to be baptized, and Dylan is the name I will give him.' So they had the boy baptized, and as they baptized him he plunged into the sea. And immediately when he was in the sea, he took its nature, and swam as well as the best fish that was therein. And for that reason was he called Dylan, the son of the Wave.

The Mabinogion translated by Lady Charlotte Guest.

Arianrhod had been summoned before Math, the King, to act as a serving maiden, for Math could live only if his feet were in the lap of a maiden. However, she bore a child, Dylan, who, once baptized, disappeared into the sea.

This tale is one of four in *The Mabinogion*. The earliest written version is in *Llyfr Gwyn Rhydderch* (The White Book of Rhydderch) at the National Library of Wales, Aberystwyth, and it probably dates from around 1300.

The story itself dates from prehistory and may deal with ancient Celtic Gods. While Dylan is little known today, his brother Lugh – Lleu in Welsh – is still remembered in place names such as Leyden, Caerliwelydd (Carlisle), Lyon, known to the Romans as Lugudunum, and Bologna, all of which were particularly associated with the worship of Lugh.

minutes from traditional agricultural communities, from farmers and fishermen, from cockle-pickers and gatherers of seaweed for the local speciality of laver-bread. It was also minutes from steelworks and coalmines and copper works and a sprawling industrial area that showed the worst of industrial, urban development. Swansea was, and is, both Welsh and English, both rural and industrial, modern and ancient; isolated and yet a busy port in contact with the world.

Dylan's paternal grandparents lived in rural, Welsh-speaking, chapel-going Carmarthenshire, but his father had left to study English at university and had then moved to Swansea to teach English at the Grammar School. His maternal grandparents had moved from Carmarthenshire to seek work on the railways, so Dylan's mother had been born in Swansea.

Welsh was the first language of both families, but Dylan was brought up to speak only English – and to speak it with a strange, plum-in-the-mouth accent. If David John meant the names of his son to be significant, to be a challenge to the future, he equipped his son to deliver that challenge only in the English language, and not in the language of his fathers.

D. J. Thomas, Dylan's father.

Florence Thomas, Dylan's mother.

Davies Brothers, Fruit and Game Merchants, in the Uplands.

Dylan grew up between two different worlds, and between two very different parents. His father was a frustrated and angry would-be poet disguised as a provincial school-teacher in a respectable semi-detached house in a respectable middle-class suburb. He could be contemptuous, irritable, violent and aggressive, and escape was often found in alcohol. Nevertheless, he was remembered by many pupils as an effective and powerful teacher, and the relationship between him and Dylan seems always to have remained strong and deep.

His mother was less complex: she appears to have been a happier and more radiant person who showered her children with love and care – perhaps to excess, for she is thought to have so spoiled her pretty, curly-haired son that she may have provoked many of his difficulties in dealing with the world in later life.

These divisions and conflicts between two ways of life, two languages, and two quite different temperaments caused tensions that were important throughout Dylan's life.

II

Dylan, of course, as a child was blissfully unaware of these facts. More immediately important to him was that he had lovely blond curls, that he was bright and pretty, that he had an elder sister, a live-in maid and a doting mother to attend to him. He was also rather sickly and his mother lavished unquestioningly her care and attention on this wonderful curly-headed angel. She was so protective that she kept him away from school altogether until he was seven, and even after that, she was always ready to believe that there was something wrong with him, always ready to nurse and look after him, always ready to spoil and to pamper.

Remarkably enough, this poor health seems to have interfered only with the less pleasant parts of life, such as school and obligations. When it came to playing in Cwmdonkin Park, the wonderland just across the street from his house, to chasing and fighting with other children, to holidays, his health seemed rather robust.

a respectable, semi-detached house . . . in a respectable middle-class suburb.
5 Cwmdonkin Drive

This photo from 1910 shows the new suburb for the middle classes which had only recently been developed when the Thomases moved into their house in 1914.

He learned early that one advantage of being a curly-headed angel is that you can get away with a lot in life. His mother also taught him that by pleading illness he could avoid the unpleasantness of the world. So he discovered that work, routine and obligations could be dodged, and that a mother figure could wave a magic wand and kiss everything better.

Dylan made much in his life of being ill, claiming all sorts of interesting diseases, from consumption to cirrhosis. Even in later life, he escaped reality by retiring to bed 'unwell', and having his favourite treats from childhood, sugared bread and milk, brought to his sick-bed. As he never became keen on work, routine and obligations, he had frequent recourse both to feigned sickness and to a series of mother-friend-wife-lover figures with magic wands.

Perhaps because of this protected childhood, Dylan Thomas always dreamed of a Paradise in which he could escape the harsh reality of life, and this dream was always set in the places of his childhood, and especially in Cwmdonkin Park and in Fern Hill. He summoned up this dreamworld in both poems and stories that are among the most powerful and evocative descriptions of the wonder of childhood ever written. In 'A Child's Christmas in Wales' and in 'A Story', two short stories inspired by his mother's family in St Thomas, Swansea, and especially in his poem 'Fern Hill', he succeeds in recreating the innocence of the child, the freshness of the world, and a sense of wonder and awe which so quickly fades.

Fern Hill is a farm near Llangain, Carmarthenshire, where his Uncle Jack and Auntie Ann lived, and where Dylan spent various holidays. 'Fern Hill' is perhaps the most popular and one of the most complete poems that Dylan ever wrote. In the poem he conjures up the wonder of childhood by describing the child playing in the farm, at one with the glorious light-filled world around him, falling asleep as the owls swoop and hoot, then waking, innocent, fresh, to the wonders of the world, like Adam on the first day in Eden.

Yet Fern Hill, like Eden, contains the seed of destruction, for while the child plays, even then, time is passing. The child is heading inexorably, green and dying, towards the end of time.

The celebrating nature of the poem comes from the fact that the child is not conscious of any restraints, nor of death, and can 'sing' in his chains, like the sea.

III

In 1925 Dylan entered Swansea Grammar School, where his father was the Senior English master. Dylan always claimed that he had not had a proper education, and his poor academic record was no doubt a result of both his own shortcomings and the lax discipline of the school – made worse, of course, by his inevitable 'illness' whenever exams came around.

In English, however, he excelled. His father had been reading Shakespeare to him from a very tender age, and Dylan had started writing poetry at the age of eight or nine. At the Grammar School he started to write poems and pieces for the school magazine and went on to be the editor. Many of the early pieces were comic, and his gift as a comic writer was to come to the fore again in later life with his stories and with *Under Milk Wood*.

His other main interest was the theatre, and he performed in school plays and then in various amateur productions over a number of years at the Swansea Little Theatre. He was generally thought to be very successful, if somewhat over-exuberant, as an actor, and these talents stood him in good stead in his later work for the B.B.C. and in his reading tours of the United States. The performance of words in the theatre can only have reinforced his fascination with the sounds and the music of words in his poetry.

a child's christmas in wales

Years and years and years ago, when I was a boy, when
there were wolves in Wales, and birds the colour of red-
flannel petticoats whisked past the harp-shaped hills, when
we sang and wallowed all night and day in caves that smelt
like Sunday afternoons in damp front farmhouse parlours,
and we chased, with the jawbones of deacons, the English
and the bears, before the motor-car, before the wheel,
before the duchess-faced horse, when we rode the daft
and happy hills bareback, it snowed and it snowed.

'A Child's Christmas in Wales' is one of Dylan Thomas's most popular
pieces. It describes Christmas Day with his mother's family in Swansea.
In contrast to the chattering, snoring, scurrying, tippling adults, the
children go out to explore. They discover wolves and snow like
mountains and frozen seas and mysterious, frightening voices that
send them racing back to the warmth and safety of the family.

1

In 1931 he left school, and started work at the *South Wales Daily Post* as a proof-reader and then as a reporter. He was not, however, particularly good at this job and the employment was ended after about eighteen months in December 1932. Apart from a period as a script-writer for propaganda films during the war, he was never to have a job again.

Through school, the theatre and work, Dylan acquired a circle of close friends who were as passionate about art as he was. Mervyn Levy and Fred Janes were painters; Daniel Jones and Tom Warner were musicians; Charles Fisher, Trevor Hughes and Bert Trick were writers. They met to talk and to discuss each other's work in homes and in pubs, and especially in the coffee house which gave its name to Swansea's famous 'Kardomah gang'.

Dylan continued to write and to become increasingly obsessed by writing. He seems never to have considered any other life or work apart from that of a poet. From 1930 to 1934, between the ages of 16 and 20, he wrote some two hundred and fifty poems, including early versions of more than half the poems he ever published, and virtually all the poems in his first two books. He also wrote short stories, such as 'The Map of Love' and 'A Prospect of the Sea', several of which were published in later volumes.

The major subjects which dominated his work – life, death, creativity and destruction – are apparent even in these earliest poems. His preoccupation with death came perhaps because he believed, or at least played at believing, that he did not have long to live.

He argued that life cannot exist without death, nor death without life, and so both are complementary expressions of the same force, the force that both creates and destroys. Children may be ignorant of this grim alliance, as has been seen in 'Fern Hill', but nobody can escape this ineluctable fact. In what is perhaps the best known poem of his first collection, Dylan wrote,

'The force that through the green fuse drives the flower / Drives my green age'.

In this vision of a universe fired by one elemental energy, the individual is only a small and insignificant part of a cosmic, eternal order. The individual dies, but life is unending, repeated forever in the cycle of sex, birth, life and death. Dylan wrote in his first poem published in London, 'Though lovers be lost, love shall not'. Life renews itself always – 'And death shall have no dominion'.

Cwmdonkin Park, 1910, the urban setting for impossible dreams.

'The ugly . . .

The North Dock and The Island, Swansea, c 1915.

Between leaving school in 1931 and moving to London in November 1934, life for Dylan in Cwmdonkin Drive changed dramatically, in some ways for the better; mainly for the worse.

His sister Nancy married and moved to London in May 1933; many of Dylan's schoolboy friends had also gone to London or to other cities to study or to work. His father had cancer and at the time was given only a few years to live. With his father unable to

. . . lovely town.'

Today Swansea sits comfortably astride different worlds and different cultures.

work, there was even less money than usual and his parents planned to sell Cwmdonkin Drive and move to a smaller house. Life at home, as described by his sister in her letters, sounds like some awful hell, where poverty, drunkenness, violence, aggression and jealousy bred.

Even the refuge of Fern Hill had gone, for his 'ancient peasant' Aunt Ann had died of cancer earlier that year: her funeral is recorded in the poem 'After the Funeral'.

pamela hansford johnson

Born in 1912, Pamela Hansford Johnson lived and worked during her early life in Clapham. Her first volume of poetry was published in 1932. Between 1933 and 1935 she maintained a close relationship with Dylan Thomas and they thought of marriage.

In 1935 her first novel was published and met with critical success.

After Dylan had stayed with her and her mother in Battersea on several occasions, and after a more significant and unhappy visit to Swansea, she realized that Dylan was not the most suitable person for a husband and the relationship was broken off.

Pamela Hansford Johnson has written many successful novels and several perceptive works of criticism.

In 1950 she married the eminent scientist and novelist C. P. Snow, later Sir and then Lord Snow, author of *Corridors of Power* and a Minister in the Labour government of 1964.

It is against this bleak background that Dylan emerged as a poet of real talent and worth. In May 1933 'And death shall have no dominion' appeared in the *New English Weekly* – his first poem to be published in London. In the same year he had a poem read on the B.B.C., various other poems were printed in London, and, in September 1933, 'That sanity be kept' was published in *The Sunday Referee*.

The publication of that poem prompted a letter of support from Pamela Hansford Johnson, a young writer in London who had already had several poems published in *The Sunday Referee*. Dylan was immediately flattered by the attention of such an attractive young woman and their relationship developed by means of sometimes flirtatious, often intense and philosophical correspondence.

By the end of the year, Dylan was becoming well known in literary circles in London and he could be reasonably hopeful of having his poems published in certain magazines and papers, even if they were not always the ones he would have chosen. In 1933 he visited London for the first time and made contact with several important writers and editors.

Other visits to London followed quickly. Sometimes he stayed with his sister, sometimes with Pamela Hansford Johnson and her mother, for romance had blossomed between the two young poets.

For Pamela and Wynd and Mrs. J. with all my love Dylan. Christmas 1936 but the photograph's earlier? hope x

1

However, Pamela Hansford Johnson was apprehensive about Dylan and about the wayward behaviour that resulted from his drinking. As a result of her fears, she rejected Dylan's proposal of marriage in June 1934. Their relationship cooled even more after an unhappy visit she made with her mother to the Thomas family in Swansea in September, 1934. The relationship limped on into 1935, but it was only a matter of time until they finally called it off.

In March, 1934, a fuss over an allegedly obscene poem published in *The Listener* made him better known, and, in April 1934, it was announced that he had won the annual Poet's Corner prize awarded by *The Sunday Referee*. The prize was the turning point in his life, for it led to the publication of his first collection: *Eighteen Poems*. Within a short time of winning the prize, he had a literary agent who wanted to sell his stories and a projected novel; he was reviewing books for magazines; more and more people were interested in his poems; he was even earning a little money.

Swansea offered less and less, while London promised more and more. Still terribly shy, intellectually, socially, sexually frustrated, without work or money, Dylan could no longer find his place in the petty, provincial, puritanical world of Wales. He was now a well-known poet, praised by world-famous artists, sought out by editors and critics, and though he had no job, no prospect of money, and nowhere to live in the city, still London beckoned.

He was only nineteen.

The fact that he never found his place outside Wales led to the tragedy of his life, but we shall come to that later.

CHAPTER TWO

Peace and War

Wales and England

1932 – 1949

Poison or grapes

The year before he left Swansea for the first time, Dylan wrote the poem 'Ears in the Turrets hear' from which the title of this chapter is taken. In this poem, he tried to peer into the future, wondering about leaving the security of the world he knew for the wide world outside. The young man, uncertain, afraid, eager, wonders whether the outside world would threaten and overwhelm him or whether it would enrich and liberate him. Should he welcome the unknown or keep the door firmly shut against it? Would it offer poison or grapes?

This question haunted him throughout the next period of his life. It was a question to which he never found the answer.

For seventeen years Dylan led a very unsettled life, moving from house to house, from town to town. He was pulled constantly between Wales and London, satisfied in neither place, always longing for the other as soon as he was in one. During this time, between the ages of eighteen and thirty-five, he married, had three children, progressed from a penniless young poet to a major media figure, a broadcaster, film-writer, earning very large sums of money, world famous: fêted. Fated.

Although the external circumstances changed enormously, many aspects of his life continued as before. He remained dependent and irresponsible, careless of material possessions and of money, regardless of whether the possessions and money belonged to him or to somebody else. He remained irresistible to friends and admirers, sought after by editors and broadcasters. He remained deeply and passionately attached to his father, and to his wife with whom he loved and fought in often public and spectacular brawls and reconciliations. He still relied on others to look after him in both the tedious details of everyday life and in major questions of family and financial security. He still drank too much. At times he lied and he stole.

Most important, he still wrote; but mainly only when he was in Wales.

The Mumbles: Dylan's favourite haunt in Swansea

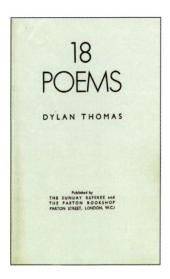

I

In December 1934, *18 poems* was published. The months following publication saw the book reviewed in many magazines, and the reviews were generally favourable, if not ecstatic. A new poet had been launched.

In the autumn of 1934 Dylan moved to London. He shared rooms in a boarding house near Earl's Court with his Swansea friends Fred Janes and Mervyn Levy. However, he did not stay there for long at any one time, and he returned to Swansea frequently and for long periods.

On a superficial level, his life became a round of meetings with editors, of attempts to write, of shuttling back and forth between Swansea and London, of drunken and boyish outings with his friends to pubs and dances in the 'bohemian' worlds of Chelsea and Soho, and of random, immature sexual experiences both within and without the bounds of what was then considered 'normal' behaviour. A casualty of this uncontrolled life was his relationship with Pamela Hansford Johnson which finally came to an end in early 1935.

By the time he was twenty, many of the characteristics that were both to serve him and to destroy him were much in evidence. He had great difficulty in coping with life and in managing to behave in a way that was socially acceptable – even by the lax standards allowed to poets and artists.

Perhaps it was a deep-rooted and unconquerable feeling of insecurity, perhaps an absolute inner conviction that he could never, should never succeed that led him into those inappropriate behaviour patterns that dogged him throughout his life, and right up to his very last words before his death: 'I've drunk eighteen straight whiskies. I think that's the record'.

Perhaps it was because he was used to being pampered by his mother that he continually sought other women to mother him, which led him into the most impossible, baby-like behaviour, often at the most unfortunate times.

Whatever the reasons, he became increasingly unreliable and dishonest – and entirely self-centred. Of course, these faults were aggravated by his drinking: it may be that he drank much less than rumour has it – but no matter how much it actually was, it was too much for him.

At a deeper level, the only level he cared about, he was a poet. He was driven on by the belief that his destiny was to be a poet and nothing else. He was a meticulous craftsman, working and re-working his poems, sometimes hundreds of times, spending, so he claimed, days on one line. He was a daring, innovative poet who wrote what he wanted to write, regardless of fashion or commercial considerations.

During this first period in London he made many new friends and acquaintances, some of whom stayed faithful throughout his life; some of whom quickly parted company with this rather wayward genius: Geoffrey Grigson, a poet and the dynamic editor of *New Verse* and an early publisher of Dylan's poems;

the hunchback in the park

Like the park birds he came early
Like the water he sat down
And Mister they called Hey mister
The truant boys from the town
Running when he had heard them clearly
On out of sound.

This poem describes a hunchback who spends his days, from early morning until nightfall, in Cwmdonkin Park.

At first the hunchback is described as others see him: a lonely figure huddled on a bench, persecuted and taunted by the world around him. Then we are shown the dreams which fill the hunchback's days: dreams of perfection and beauty, of a woman as straight and as tall as the hunchback is crooked and bent.

When night falls the park is locked, and boys, lovers and the hunchback are all cast out from this Eden. All that remains in the park is the notion of perfection that the hunchback had called up.

This poem was written in 1941 and was a re-worked version of a poem first developed in his notebooks in 1932. It was published in *Deaths and Entrances* in 1946.

Victor Neuberg, a middle-aged eccentric and the editor of Poet's Corner in *The Sunday Referee* who had been Dylan's first supporter; Cyril Connolly, then a young writer and critic, destined for fame as founder of *Horizon* and as editor and reviewer for major newspapers; Rayner Heppenstall, poet, novelist, critic, broadcaster; A.J.P. Taylor, historian, academic, and his wife Margaret.

He went to stay with the Taylors in Derbyshire in early 1935, and this relationship was to remain of vital importance to him throughout his life. Margaret Taylor housed the Thomas family from early 1946 to 1953, buying various properties in Oxfordshire, in Laugharne and in London so that Dylan and his family should have somewhere to live. She supported them throughout Dylan's life, at great personal cost to herself and to her husband.

In early 1935 he returned to Swansea and met the man who was to be his most loyal friend and mentor for the rest of his life. Vernon Watkins was a poet in his own right and also contributed to the development of Dylan Thomas through his careful, meticulous and sympathetic criticisms of Dylan's writing. Virtually every piece of work that Dylan completed from the time of their meeting was sent to Vernon Watkins first, and invariably he benefited from his friend's advice and comments.

By the end of April he was back in London, but his behaviour was so self-destructive, that his friends arranged for him to go away on holiday to escape the ritual stupidity of his London life. Geoffrey Grigson took him to an isolated cottage in Ireland where Dylan started to write again. The holiday went well, but Dylan's failure to settle his bills with his Irish hosts caused an estrangement between the friends and led Grigson to reconsider his opinions of Dylan both as a man and as a poet. The outcome was a notoriously and ferociously hostile review of Dylan's next book later that year.

augustus john

Augustus John was a painter who was born in Tenby, Wales, in 1878.

He studied in London and became known as one of the most gifted and skilled painters of his day. While he continued the tradition of portrait painting, he added to it his own romantic ideas and his vigorous and individual approach.

He became a very fashionable painter of portraits and of landscapes and he undertook commissions for many leading figures of his time, including royalty and major contemporary artists. His famous portrait of Dylan is at the National Museum of Wales, Cardiff. Many of his portraits are now found in the leading art galleries of the world, including the Tate Gallery in London and the National Portrait Gallery in Washington, D.C.

The success of *18 Poems* had led Dent, a major London publishing house, to offer to publish a second collection. Dylan returned to Swansea after his Irish trip and worked on the poems, sending material to Dent piecemeal over the summer. By October he had collected what he judged to be the next collection: most were poems taken from his early Swansea notebooks, but six were new poems.

Many of these poems were even more difficult than those in *18 Poems* and Dent was uneasy about the obscurity and the sexual imagery of certain poems. The manuscript was refused. With the help and advice of Vernon Watkins, Dylan revised and reworked his poems to make them more acceptable to his new publisher.

Dylan remained in Swansea throughout the winter of 1935 – 1936, although he made frequent trips to London. He was now well established as a new poet and his poems were accepted regularly by the most prestigious magazines. In early 1936 he met Edith Sitwell who had previously written an unfavourable review of Dylan's poetry. She had changed her mind and became one of Dylan's keenest and most loyal supporters. She was such a well-known and respected figure that her support was invaluable to the young and wild poet.

For, despite his growing acceptance as a major literary figure, he remained a very wild young man. While many found Dylan entertaining, the life and soul of the party, some found his drunkenness and adolescent pranks tedious and boring.

Dylan seems already, at the age of 21, to have lost sight of the difference between fantasy and reality, between image and self. Increasingly he took on the role of the person he wanted to be, or of the person he wanted others to think he was. The person he really was disappeared from his life. This confused perception of himself and of his public persona lasted throughout his life and was perhaps the cause of his inability to live successfully.

Whatever truth there was in this confused young man appeared only in his poetry, and even there he felt obliged to hide it under endless veils of obscurity.

Dylan's life, which could not continue as it was, was about to take another, and definitive turning.

II

Chance would have it that Dylan Thomas was in a pub in London one day in 1936 when Augustus John walked in with his beautiful, eccentric companion, sometime model, sometime lover, Caitlin Macnamara. Augustus John was an extremely successful artist, who had left west Wales to become the society portrait painter of his day. He had a reputation for being overly fond of fast cars and of women. He had had many lovers and numerous children who often lived together in a lively, unconventional, extended community. Caitlin had been a member of this community for some time.

Dylan was immensely attracted by Caitlin, and competition ensued for this desirable and fiery woman between the old, rich and famous painter and the uncouth, poor, young poet.

Chance also had it that after a lengthy stay in Cornwall,

caitlin macnamara

Caitlin Macnamara was the daughter of an Irish gentleman who was cultured, educated, familiar with all the best Irish writers, and poor. Caitlin's mother was half Irish and half French and was also cultured like her husband. However, the parents divorced and Caitlin was brought up by her mother in Hampshire.

The family moved in artistic circles and were friends with Augustus John, who at one time lived close to them in Hampshire.

Caitlin was a dancer. She worked for a while at the London Palladium and her ambition was to work at the Folies Bergères, the Parisian nightspot. She had many affairs, including one with Augustus John, for whom she also posed as a model.

Caitlin had a violent temper and did not shy away from physical fights, even with men who were much bigger and stronger than she was. This characteristic continued throughout her life, and gave rise to some of the spectacular battles with Dylan that have been described by various friends.

where he was looked after by yet another substitute mother, Dylan returned to Swansea only to learn that Augustus John and Caitlin were at Laugharne, staying at the home of Richard Hughes. Dylan immediately invited himself to the house and prevailed upon his friend, Fred Janes, to drive him over one summer afternoon. An uncomfortable afternoon of bickering and tetchiness ensued as the two men quarrelled over Caitlin's attentions.

Round one of the fight between the two men was in London, and Dylan always claimed victory: he and Caitlin, so he boasted, had rushed off for a frenzied feast of sexual enjoyment as soon as they had met – although many find his claim unlikely.

Round two was in Laugharne, and the result was an incontrovertible victory for the older man. After a brawl in a pub car park in Carmarthen, a drunken and ineffectual Dylan lay in the dust while the painter and his model roared off in his car.

Round three did not take place for some ten months, not until April 1937, but by then Dylan had become a poet with two collections in print.

Despite the continued misgivings of the publishers, a compromise was reached and *25 Poems* was published in September 1936. This book met both with more success and with greater hostility, but Dylan was now

Dylan and Caitlin

well established and his reputation assured. Moreover, the book sold well, largely thanks to Edith Sitwell's prominent and enthusiastic support: the Dylan Thomas phenomenon had started. He was, and he remains, a difficult, obscure poet whose work, nevertheless, appeals to a wide audience.

However, the financial returns, even for a best-selling poet, were small and he soon returned to Swansea.

richard hughes

Born 1900 in Kent of a Welsh family, Richard Hughes was a playwright, a poet, an essayist and a novelist.

While still a student at Oxford he had a short play produced in London and was praised by G. B. Shaw. In 1922 he also published a volume of poems, while in 1929 his best known novel *A High Wind in Jamaica* appeared.

His wife, Frances, was a cousin of Lady Marged Howard-Stepney, the only daughter of a rich family of landowners in Carmarthenshire, an eccentric and rather wayward figure in her own right, and an enthusiastic and generous supporter of Dylan Thomas.

In early 1937 he was back in London and then he and Caitlin went to Cornwall together. His description of his future wife is a proud, defiant statement of her qualities, and especially of her total disregard for money and material possessions: '[Caitlin is] sufficiently like myself to care little or nothing for proprietary interests and absolutely nothing for the responsibilities of husbandly provision.' Far from correcting each other's excesses, they shared and encouraged them. It is hard to imagine a spirit so free as to criticize Dylan for being turgidly middle class and materialistic. Caitlin was such a rare free spirit. Unfortunately, the fine, if unconventional qualities that they shared were to lead to tragedy, not to happiness.

They were married in July 1937 despite considerable opposition from Dylan's family. They stayed on in borrowed accommodation in Cornwall for a while, often in the company of friends and of other artists who were holidaying in neighbouring villages. Later that year they stayed with Dylan's parents in Bishopston and then they went for six months to Caitlin's mother's in Hampshire. In May 1938 they again returned to Dylan's parents in Bishopston and then they went on to the village that was to become so important in their lives: Laugharne. At first they moved into a cottage that Richard Hughes had found for them, and then into Sea View, a house between the castle and the sea, overlooking the beach and the estuary.

Dylan, Caitlin and J. C. Wyn Lewis at Rhosili.

*Laugharne Castle.
It was in the summerhouse of
the castle, looking out over the
estuary, that Dylan completed
one of his best loved poems,
'The Hunchback in the Park'.*

This first period in Laugharne was perhaps the happiest
that the Thomas family ever knew. Although Caitlin and Dylan
argued, the reconciliations followed quickly. Dylan was writing
again, both poems and stories, stories that were very different
from anything he had done before. Now he wrote about people
he had known and he dealt with real situations and emotions in
a generally compassionate and humorous way. When they were
published in 1940 as *Portrait of the Artist as a Young Dog* they
established Dylan Thomas as a fine writer of stories and of
humorous sketches.

By 1938 Dylan was discussing publication in America, and
money was received from supporters there, as well as from many
in Britain. However, a collection of early stories that was to have
been published and on which he had counted to provide money
was abandoned, for the publisher was afraid of being prosecuted for
obscenity, and the money that his poetry produced was very little.

As Dylan and Caitlin shared the weaknesses of irresponsibility
and an almost total inability to think ahead, they were always
short of money. It was not that money did not come in: it was
that no matter how quickly money came in, it always went out
more quickly.

Eventually they owed so much to so many people in the village of Laugharne that, in October 1938, they moved out and returned to Caitlin's mother's house, where they spent the next winter.

In April 1939 they returned to Wales, now with their first child, Llywelyn. The desperate need for refuge was reinforced by threats of war and by Dylan's distress at the possibility of being drafted into the Army. He spent a lot of time trying to find a way to avoid military service. He explored the possibility of being a conscientious objector, either on religious or political grounds, and of volunteering for a position in a special section of the army reserved for artists. All these possibilities came to nothing. Given Dylan's record of pleading illness whenever he wanted to avoid something unpleasant, it is ironic that at this stage of his life he did not plead ill health -only to be rejected as physically unfit for active service by the Army!

The war also aggravated his financial problems. *The Map of Love*, a collection of 15 poems and 5 stories, was published by Dent in August 1939 and received generally positive reviews. On 3rd September, war was declared and the book was forgotten. In the same way, *Portrait of the Artist as a Young Dog* was published in April 1940 and was a commercial failure, despite the favourable reviews and the more accessible quality of this collection of stories about his own childhood.

Debts again drove them from Laugharne in the autumn of 1939 and they escaped to Caitlin's mother. They came back to Laugharne in the spring of 1940, but again quickly fled their debts, this time retreating to Dylan's parents in Swansea.

They were then invited to the house of a friend in Gloucestershire. John Davenport, an ex-boxer, an ex-poet, an ex-Hollywood scriptwriter, a collector of fine wines and fine paintings, was defiantly and resolutely spending his fortune before the war could take it from him. As the war clouds gathered, he assembled a party of house-guests that included musicians and writers who were staying at his house indefinitely. As the bombs fell on London and Swansea, art, intrigue and infidelity flourished in this 'gilded cage', as Caitlin called it.

Yet although Dylan was terrified of the war, other fears went even deeper, for he abandoned this haven when he suspected Caitlin of having an affair with one of the other guests. Perhaps, as many critics claim, he really was more 'Swansea middle-class' than 'international bohemian'.

It is from such unpleasant situations that the germ of the idea of *Under Milk Wood* grew. Dylan loathed and feared the war. Confronted with the horror around him, he imagined a place that would turn aside from this frightful carnage, a place sane enough to reject the insanity of the rest of the world. Of course, a person who believes something fundamentally different from the rest of the world is quickly labelled as insane, no matter how sane he might consider himself. So, Dylan reasoned, the only sane village in the world would be declared insane, and *The Town that was Mad* was the ironic working title for the ideas that finally surfaced in *Under Milk Wood*.

When they left John Davenport's house, they returned to Swansea. Then, in February, 1941, Swansea underwent three successive nights of bombing and much of the city was destroyed. Dylan's parents planned to leave the city for the country near Llansteffan. Dylan and Caitlin went back again to Laugharne, this time to Richard Hughes's house next to the castle itself. It is there that he wrote the last poem to be taken from his early notebooks, for he now sold these manuscripts in order to survive for another few weeks. He also tried to make money by writing an autobiographical novel, *Adventures in the Skin Trade*. The project foundered, however, both because Dylan could not take this hack work seriously, and because his publishers wrote a very firm and severe rejection after they had seen the first chapters.

During much of the early period of the war, Dylan had been trying to find protected work for the government or the B.B.C.. Late in 1941 he was offered a job as a script-writer for a film company working for the Ministry of Information. He was well paid, had regular employment, could work when and where he wanted, was surrounded by interesting and lively people. Life could, should have been easy for him!

In this way, it was the war that provided Dylan with the basis of what should have been a comfortable financial situation. Money came in ever greater amounts. Yet he continued to steal, to beg and to plead poverty, taking from those with much less than he had. This behaviour must have had less to do with money itself than with other, deeper aspects of his character, perhaps with his compelling need to force others to pay attention to and to look after the perpetual spoiled child; perhaps with a need to fail, even when fame and fortune stared him in the face.

Dylan and Caitlin now moved frequently from London to Wales and back again, sometimes together, sometimes apart, and, in Dylan's case at least, sometimes fleetingly with other partners. Much of 1942 was spent in Talsarn, near Lampeter, in the house of Vera, one of Dylan's childhood friends. Early 1943, when their daughter Aeron was born, was spent in Chelsea. Then it was back to Wales, then London, then in early 1944 Sussex, then to Beaconsfield. In July they moved back to Wales, to the cottage in Llangain where his parents now lived, and the poetry began to flow again.

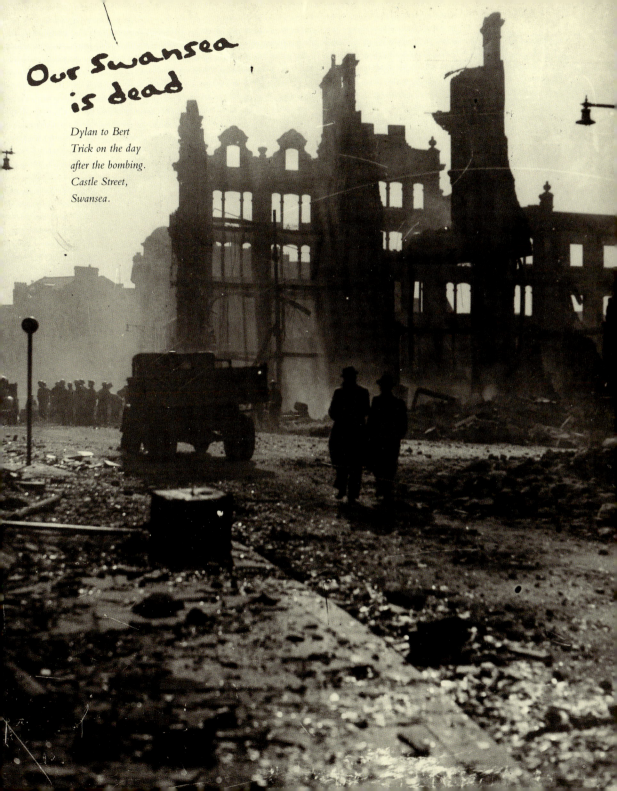

Our Swansea is dead

Dylan to Bert Trick on the day after the bombing. Castle Street, Swansea.

Oxford Street. Swansea,
22 February, 1941.

a refusal to mourn the death, by fire, of a child in london

Deep with the first dead lies London's daughter,

Robed in the long friends,

The grains beyond age, the dark veins of her mother,

Secret by the unmourning water

Of the riding Thames.

After the first death, there is no other.

Both Dylan and Caitlin wanted to move back to Laugharne, but could not find rooms to rent and so, in September 1944, they went to New Quay instead, to a bungalow next door to the same Vera whose house they had shared in Talsarn. Dylan was away for much of the time, and life at home was more and more difficult. This period of their lives culminated in an infamous episode in which Vera's husband, a war-weary commando freshly back from the horrors of the war in Greece, was provoked beyond measure by Dylan's entourage from the world of films. His fury, fuelled by politics, grief, jealousy and the suspicion of sexual infidelities, led to a shooting incident and to charges of attempted murder that, in the end, came to nothing.

The return to Wales had, however, stimulated a surge of activity which produced more poems in a short period than at any time since his early days in Swansea. Not only did he rediscover his gifts, but he found gifts that were more profound and richer than anything that had gone before. In one short period, he wrote many of those poems which have ensured his position as a great poet despite all the scandal and despite all his detractors: 'Poem in October', 'A Refusal to Mourn the Death, by Fire, of a Child in London', 'The Conversation of Prayers', 'In my craft or sullen art', and 'Fern Hill'. Dylan, settled in Wales, had come of age and produced the work which he had always promised. Unfortunately, this rich spell was not to last and in the remaining eight years of his life he wrote only another eight poems.

He also wrote radio talks: 'Quite Early One Morning', a precursor of *Under Milk Wood*, and 'Memories of Christmas', the first version of what was to become his best known and most loved prose piece, 'A Child's Christmas in Wales'. As the war dragged on, Dylan worked a vein of nostalgia and of regret for the innocence and fantasy of childhood that, rightly or wrongly, has outlasted much of his more difficult and intellectual work.

poem in october

It was my thirtieth year to heaven
Woke to my hearing from harbour and neighbour wood
And the mussel pooled and the heron
Priested shore
The morning beckon
With water praying and call of seagull and rook
And the knock of sailing boats on the net webbed wall
Myself to set foot
That second
In the still sleeping town and set forth.

When the new poems were published in *Deaths and Entrances* in 1946 they met with great acclaim and finally established beyond doubt Dylan's position as a major poet. The first edition sold out immediately and the publisher not only reprinted this new book, but also re-issued his earlier volumes. Finally commercial success beckoned.

III

From 1945 to 1949 Dylan and Caitlin lived almost exclusively in England, not out of choice, but because somebody else was willing to look after them. After a winter in London, they arrived, unannounced, homeless, penniless, on the doorstep of Margaret Taylor in Oxford in early 1946 and she became the patron that Dylan wanted. At first she gave them a summer house in the garden to live in, and when they no longer liked that, she bought a house for them near Oxford. In 1948 Dylan's parents also moved into this house. When they no longer liked that house, she bought the Boat House in Laugharne. When they wanted something else, she bought a place in London.

Such generosity saved the Thomases, but did nothing to help personal relationships. A.J.P. Taylor did not share his wife's besotted attitude, and could not stand the noisy, brawling Thomas family and their endless demands for money. Caitlin was jealous of Margaret Taylor, both of her money and of her possessive, patronising attitude. Dylan and Caitlin drank and fought more and more. The Taylors eventually divorced.

Dylan did not feel settled in England and was always trying to escape to the United States. He bombarded all those he thought might help him with letters asking about the possibility of moving to America permanently, about jobs as a writer, poet, teacher, broadcaster. Nothing came of his enquiries but the idea remained in his head and surfaced, in a different form, in his subsequent trips to America.

After the end of the war, his job as a script-writer ended. Dylan now turned increasingly to the B.B.C. and he became a contributor to a wide variety of programmes, as a writer, and more and more as a speaker and actor. His drink problem was such, however, that the B.B.C. would not consider anything more than casual employment, and even then they had doubts about him. He was, however, very successful and very popular, and he was well paid and well treated. In 1947 he wrote 'Return Journey' for the B.B.C., a subtle and engaging piece about the life he may once have had, but which had disappeared as surely and as finally as the streets of Swansea: both that life and the streets now lay in rubble.

For despite the unfailing, if perhaps misguided generosity of Margaret Taylor and of many other supporters such as Edith Sitwell, Dylan was not well and was deteriorating. In 1947, he was given money to go away to Italy for three months, but he does not seem to have enjoyed or benefited from his period, although he did write a little while he was there.

Later that year he was commissioned to write a film script, and that led to other scripts and finally to regular commissions in 1948. He was now very highly regarded both as broadcaster and as script-writer and was very highly paid. Such things mean nothing, though, in the life of Dylan, for no matter how much money he earned, he never had any.

Then, in 1949, his script-writing came to an end. His parents had moved into the house in Oxford with them, and created many other problems. He was also in debt to the Inland Revenue for unpaid Income Tax and the B.B.C. had had enough of his antics.

It was time for him to run away again. For the last time.

In 1949 he found the refuge that sheltered him for the last few years of his life.

The view from
The Boat House

CHAPTER **3** *THREE*

Success and failure

Laugharne and

the United States

1949 – 1953

Fathered and found

Over the last four years of his life, the contradictory impulses in Dylan Thomas became even more pronounced.

On the one hand, his reputation as a major poet and performer was beyond question. He toured the United States, rubbing shoulders with the great figures of both the cultural and the entertainment worlds, from Stravinsky to Chaplin, from Lotte Lenya to Marilyn Monroe. He earned well and the promise of even greater fame and fortune was in his grasp.

On the other hand, his marriage seemed beyond hope as he embarked on various affairs and as he left his family in poverty in Laugharne while he travelled the world as a star. He was also afraid that he had lost his inspiration, and that he had nothing more to say as a poet.

At times, his behaviour was so appalling that people shunned him. At times, his behaviour was so charming, so vital, that he was sought out and lionized.

His whole being was torn in different ways: something had to give.

The Boat House, Laugharne

After the war, in the few years left to him, Dylan wrote only some seven or so new poems: 'Over Sir John's Hill', 'Poem on His Birthday', 'Do not go gentle into that good night', 'Lament', 'In the White Giant's Thigh', 'In Country Heaven', 'Elegy' (unfinished). They are among the most profound, the most brilliant of his life. He was also to write various scripts and prose pieces and his play for voices, *Under Milk Wood*.

Dylan and Caitlin moved from Oxford to Laugharne in the spring of 1949, to the Boat House which Margaret Taylor had bought for them. Dylan's parents, who had been living with them in Oxfordshire, moved to The Pelican, a cottage they had rented on the main street in Laugharne. Caitlin was pregnant again, and Colm was born in July.

*Interior of
The Boat House*

Almost immediately Dylan began to write, using the shed alongside the path that led from the village to the house as his place of work. The first poem he wrote there was 'Over Sir John's Hill', written within a few weeks of moving and inspired by the view from the window of his shed. In this powerful and poignant poem, Dylan describes the hawk and heron as they stalk their prey, calling the innocent to death at dusk. Dylan saw life, death and God in all their mysterious, blood-stained glory in the view from the shed perched on the cliff above the estuary

Chance would have it that in that same month, just as he rediscovered the vitality of his creative urge, he achieved something for which he had yearned for years, but which had already become an almost forgotten dream: he was invited to go to the United

States to read and to lecture. The urgent renewal of life in his poetry and the potentially destructive temptations that awaited him in New York came pushing their faces against his shed window at the same time. Tragically, the force of destruction won over the force of creation.

John Malcolm Brinnin was a poet himself and a long-time admirer of Dylan's poetry. He had recently been appointed to a senior position in the Young Men's and Young Women's Hebrew Association in New York. One of his first acts as Director was to invite Dylan to New York to read at the Hebrew Association's Centre, for which he offered a fee of $500, and expenses. This was more than Dylan earned from the publication of his poetry by Dent in his whole lifetime; more than he earned for complete playscripts and acting jobs at the B.B.C.. Brinnin also offered to arrange readings and lectures in other centres.

Needless to say, Dylan wrote back promptly and accepted the offer. He would, he said, go to the States for two to three months in the spring of 1950. He calculated that such a trip would solve his financial problems for ever and allow him to write calmly, able to refuse the commissioned work that he did to make ends meet. Caitlin was to stay in Laugharne with children and parents-in-law.

However, there were the intervening months to get through, and ends were again stubbornly refusing to meet. He gave after-dinner addresses to clubs and societies; he read for the B.B.C., although it irked him that the B.B.C. had decided not to pay him in advance any more, for in recent years he had frequently taken money and failed to produce the scripts for which he had been paid. Once more, he wrote begging letters.

Exterior of the shed

Interior of the shed

Dylan in New York

In February, 1950 he left for New York. For three months he criss-crossed the States. From New York to New England to Baltimore to Ohio to Chicago to San Francisco to Vancouver to Los Angeles to New York to Michigan and to New York – although he himself rarely seemed to know or care where he was.

In New York a relationship developed that was to threaten his marriage and his tranquillity in the years to come. While there may or may not have been other casual sexual encounters during the trip, this affair was deeper and Dylan was profoundly drawn to his new partner. Although Dylan and his lover were to meet later in 1950 in London, in May the poet was ready to go home.

He left New York by ship at the end of May

The tour had been successful in many ways: Dylan read and performed (almost) faultlessly, turning up on time, holding audiences of up to a thousand spellbound by the power of his readings of a wide and fascinating selection of poetry; Dylan had showed himself to be a performer, and an outlet for his talents had been found. He had made many friends, and had met many people.

Unfortunately, Dylan was not a good traveller. His first trip abroad had been to Italy in 1947, and he had spent much of his time huddled in a house near Florence, complaining that there was no beer and listening to cricket commentaries on the B.B.C. World Service. He seems to have shown interest neither in Florence, one of the most spectacular cities in the world, nor in the life and people of Italy. A subsequent trip to Prague does not reveal him as any better fitted to leave the little patch in which he had grown up.

In America he seems to have adopted the reactions of many poor travellers: just as some people seem to believe that a foreigner will somehow understand your language if you shout loud enough, so some believe that it is not necessary to observe the niceties of normal behaviour and speech when abroad. Dylan seems to have been such a traveller, and in that his behaviour and speech often

3

left much to be desired even at home, it is not surprising that in America he sometimes dismayed and appalled his hosts. He was at times aggressive, rude, drunk, lecherous, uncouth, coarse, and he made many enemies.

Was this the 'real' Dylan Thomas free to express himself far away from the restrictions of home? Was this a front behind which the real man could hide his insecurity, his uncertainty and the fear of a naive and unworldly innocent in strange waters? Nobody knows. Nobody can ever know. Whatever truth there may have been has been buried under layers of either legend or whitewash ever since.

On a much more basic and concrete level, the tour was a dreadful fiasco in that the reason for the tour had been to make money, and in that Dylan returned home with virtually nothing in his pocket. His wife and three children had waited, penniless and virtually destitute, living off the charity of others, in Laugharne

The Mermaid Hotel, Mumbles, was Dylan's favourite pub as a young man in Swansea.

while Dylan roared across America. Yet the golden eggs that America provided were also devoured far away in the bleak anonymity of foreign parts. Dylan and Caitlin had fantasized about the 'lovely desert islands' which would be the fruit of his American tour. This fantasy now gave way to the reality that they were still trapped, penniless and unhappy, in the 'moist, smothering, lost boghole' of Laugharne.

In the morning he called on his parents, and then he would go to Brown's to gossip, to gamble and to drink. In the afternoon, he worked on his poems in the shed, wrote begging letters to Margaret Taylor, did odd jobs for the B.B.C. In the evening, he returned to Brown's.

In this difficult period, Dylan wrote 'In the White Giant's Thigh' and 'In Country Heaven'. In an interview given in America, Dylan had said that in the future he was going to write only about 'universal happiness'. It is perhaps not surprising that while in this

'The pub was his real home.'
Gwen Watkins.

Brown's Hotel was his favourite haunt during his last years in Laugharne

The Gower.

world of acute unhappiness and uncertainty, Dylan's longing for another world of 'universal happiness' should surface again. It is this idea that had already been mentioned during the war, the dream of a parallel world where misery would be avoided. The ideas underlying *Under Milk Wood* had come to maturity, although it took some years for the play to be finished – in as much as it ever was finished.

In September, Dylan went to Brighton in the company of his lover from New York. Caitlin soon heard of this, and the marriage touched rock bottom. Towards the end of 1950 the crisis was profound and the marriage seemed to have come to an end. However, after a period of separation, when Dylan was scripting a film for BP in Persia, they decided to remain together for the moment and life took up again in Laugharne.

Amid such turmoil he managed to write 'Lament' and 'Do not go gentle into that good night'. This second poem was written when Dylan's father was desperately ill, and he expressed in it both the depth of his attachment to his father and an impassioned plea to fight the onset of death. This defiance and acceptance of death is also seen in 'Poem on his Birthday', the last completed poem he wrote, where it is the poet himself who 'sails out to die'.

The financial problems continued, despite loans and gifts, despite broadcasts, speeches, and publications. These now seemed mere crumbs to the irresponsible and ever hungry Thomases, for they now knew that real golden eggs were only in America.

It was thus decided that a second American tour was the solution to their problems, on condition that Caitlin went with him to guard against the problems that had occurred during the previous trip, especially personal entanglements with women and the strange disappearance of all the money. A worse chaperon could not be imagined.

In January 1952 they sailed for America. The route again took Dylan across the States, from New York to Arizona and California and back. Although the readings were again successful, and although Dylan's reputation in the States was continuing to grow, the trip was plagued by the same problems as before. What was worse was that Caitlin's presence, far from preventing known problems, created other and worse problems. There were now two irresponsible, drunken, brawling people to spend whatever money they earned.

Unsurprisingly, when they returned to Laugharne in June 1952, they had even more financial problems than before. By this time Margaret Taylor was running out of money and she was having to think of selling the Boat House. Dylan was failing to meet deadlines and work was drying up.

He wrote little poetry at this time. Dent had wanted to publish a volume of collected poems as early as 1950, but there had not been enough new poems to justify the volume. Even when publication had been agreed, it took Dylan almost a year to deliver the Prologue he had promised. *Collected Poems* was finally published, in November 1952, and Dylan was acclaimed as the 'greatest living poet', as 'unique'. The scope and quality of his work was now apparent and his reputation assured. Ten thousand copies of the book were sold in the first year, twenty thousand in the second in the United Kingdom alone. In the United States even more were sold.

Dylan turned once again to the project that would become *Under Milk Wood*. The idea had now been simplified, and instead of showing the 'town that was mad' in conflict with the rest of the world, he set out simply to show the town itself. So the collection of eccentric characters slowly grew and were tied together in a structure that was simple and clear: the action would cover twenty four hours in the life of the village.

The same compassion and humour that had given his short stories their inexhaustible appeal now appeared in this play. His stated intention was to write of the happiness of life, and this happiness is seen in its full glory in *Under Milk Wood*. The fear of death that gave his poems their tragic intensity disappeared.

The inhabitants of a town that was mad . . .

under milk wood

'... a piece, a play, an impression for voices ...'

Under Milk Wood grew over some twenty years. In the early 1930s he spoke of a play about Wales to take place within the space of one day. In 1939, he suggested to Richard Hughes that Laugharne needed a play in which the villagers would play themselves. The horror of war inspired the idea of *The Town that was Mad*, a picture of a village that alone remained sane in an insane world. In 1944 he wrote 'Quite Early One Morning', a radio sketch of New Quay which has many points in common with the play that finally emerged.

Under Milk Wood has always been immensely popular and successful. Within a few months of Dylan's death, the BBC had broadcast the play with Richard Burton, Hugh Griffith and Rachel Roberts among a brilliant cast of Welsh actors, and the scrpit was a best-seller in book form. Ever since, *Under Milk Wood* has continued to entertain and fascinate: it has been broadcast on the radio, made into a film, animated and performed on stage countless times by names as diverse as Sir Anthony Hopkins and Tom Jones, and there have been both pop and jazz musical versions. The play has also been translated into several languages, including Welsh.

Although Polly Garter's final, haunting song is still to little Willy Wee 'who is dead, dead, dead', this is set in a different context by the final speech in which Dylan talks of 'Heaven on Earth' and 'the innocence of men'. Although Mae Rose Cottage is hoping to sin until she blows up, she does not really believe in the notion of sin. In *Under Milk Wood*, for 'sin' read 'life'. Even if Mae Rose Cottage does blow up, even if she is as dead as the drowned sailors, as dead as Dancing Williams and Curly Bevan and Rosie Probert, she will still live in the memories and the dreams of others, in the continued frenzy of life itself.

Under Milk Wood showed the charm of a Dylan Thomas confident, secure, loving. The paradise of Fern Hill had moved a few miles across the estuary to Milk Wood, a town 'as full as a lovebird's egg'. Dylan has again managed to slip the chains of time, those chains that held him 'green and dying' at Fern Hill.

under milk wood

Captain Cat:

Who's that talking by the pump? Mrs Floyd and Boyo, talking flatfish. What can you talk about flatfish? That's Mrs Dai Bread One, waltzing up the street like a jelly, every time she shakes it's slap slap slap. Who's that? Mrs Butcher Beynon with her pet black cat, it follows her everywhere, miaow and all. There goes Mrs Twenty-Three, important, the sun gets up and goes down in her dewlap, when she shuts her eyes, it's night. High heels now, in the morning too, Mrs Rose Cottage's eldest Mae, seventeen and never been kissed ho ho, [...]. Who's having a baby, who blacked whose eye, [...], who's dead, who's dying, there's a lovely day, oh the cost of soapflakes!

3

On December 15th, 1952, Dylan's father died. This death, already foreseen in 'Do not go gentle into that good night', now inspired Dylan's last poem, 'Elegy'. This poem was incomplete when Dylan himself died, and it is fitting that it was his most loyal and inspiring friend, Vernon Watkins, who put together the version that, so he thought, was that which Dylan might have chosen.

In this subdued, muted poem, Dylan faces death yet again, a death transcended by a vaguely defined immortality in which the dead man would at last lie quietly, fathered and found. Through the contemplation of death, Dylan's vision has now become so profound and so acute that he can see to the very 'roots of the sea'. Wisdom and true knowledge had come to the poet at last. It is hard not to see in the work his own elegy, as well as that of his father.

Although Dylan may have discovered a deeper significance in life, the ordinary details continued to defeat him. He was again without money and uncertain about their future at the Boat House. Yet in early 1953 he was earning large sums of money, both for his publications, with *Collected Poems* selling very well and with royalties coming in for the use of his poems, and for his work as a performer, both live and on the radio. He had several publishing contracts lined up. He also won several cash prizes for his work. Commercial success and financial security were, in fact, being thrust upon him at this stage of his life.

Yet Dylan was to turn this success into irredeemable failure. He was not unable to earn money or success: he was unable to hold on to it. How sad it is that at the time when he was writing one of the most humorous and compassionate pictures of human life, warts and all, in *Under Milk Wood*, he seemed unable to value that work or to accept that his poetry had changed from the difficult, raw, aggressive work of his youth to the more complete view of his last poems. In his early work he spelled out the intellectual need to reconcile life and death; in his later work he had captured a

a story

But there he was, always, a steaming hulk of an uncle, his braces straining like hawsers, crammed behind the counter of the tiny shop at the front of the house, and breathing like a brass band; or guzzling and blustery in the kitchen over his gutsy supper, too big for everything except the great black boats of his boots. As he ate, the house grew smaller; he billowed out over the furniture, the loud check meadow of his waistcoat littered, as though after a picnic, with cigarette ends, peelings, cabbage stalks, birds' bones, gravy; and the forest fire of his hair crackled among the hooked hams from the ceiling. She was so small she could hit him only if she stood on a chair, and every Saturday night at half past ten he would lift her up, under his arm, on to a chair in the kitchen so that she could hit him on the head with whatever was handy, which was always a china dog. On Sundays, and when pickled, he sang high tenor, and had won many cups.

At the beginning of 'A Story', Dylan describes the home of this odd couple: the giant uncle, huffing and puffing, and the quiet, mouselike aunt.

This story describes an outing to Porthcawl, which, despite the fine sounding aims, turns out to be an epic, drunken expedition by a lot of grown men who should know better: but who don't.

3

vision in which both were reconciled. How sad to be paralysed by the fear of being unable to write, just as he had discovered a new and deeper role as a writer.

Dylan, still trying to correct his financial situation, planned another trip to America. Caitlin, who was not to accompany him this time, was most unhappy about the plan, both because she thought that these trips were bad for him as an artist, and because of his likely infidelity. They argued endlessly, but, on April 16, 1953, Dylan set sail yet again.

Llansteffan: a village to which both Dylan and his grandfather escaped at times, yet in which, so the story 'A Visit to Grandpa's' explains, his grandfather did not want to be buried, for you can't lie down without getting your feet wet!

This time he avoided the exhausting cross-country trips and performed only in the north-east. Artistically the trip was a time of great promise: an early version of *Under Milk Wood* was performed to great acclaim; he was invited to collaborate on an opera with Stravinsky. Socially it was less successful: he resumed the affair of 1950 and started another. He was drunk much too often.

In June 1953 he returned to Laugharne. He spent the summer with work for the B.B.C., with revisions to *Under Milk Wood*, and he made his first appearance on television in which he read 'A Story'. He continued to work fitfully on 'Elegy'. He wrote begging letters.

He was still confronted with the same financial problems, and so he sought the same solution: a trip to America. He had already been three times, and his problems still remained unsolved, but at least they were out of sight, and out of mind, once he was in New York. By this time he could command enormous fees for readings, and could earn the wages of the early media personality that he was. Much to Caitlin's displeasure, plans were made for another tour.

Just before his departure he delivered the final script of *Under Milk Wood* to the B.B.C.

On October 20, 1953 he arrived in New York. For fourteen days he followed a programme of working on the rehearsals of *Under Milk Wood*, interspersed with heavy bouts of drinking. He also resumed his affair, and was even unfaithful to his 'regular' lover.

Four performances of *Under Milk Wood* were given at the Poetry Centre and met with even more enthusiastic reactions than earlier that year.

For another week he went from bar to bar, from party to party and from reading to reading

On November 3rd he signed a contract with an agent for future lecture tours for which he would be handsomely paid: $1000 a week – more than a year's wage for a working man in

Britain at that time. Earning money was no longer a problem, as, indeed, it had not been a problem for several years. The real problems lay elsewhere.

On November 4th he went out to his favourite bar with his companion, but he quickly returned to his hotel, claiming that he felt unwell. A doctor was sent for and Dylan was given medication. He still felt unwell and the doctor came again and treated him again. What treatment was actually administered, and whether that treatment was correct, or in fact either contributed to or even caused his death, has been argued about ever since. The truth, as in so many other aspects of Dylan's life, will never be known. What is known is that later that evening Dylan lost consciousness. The doctor was called again and Dylan was sent to St Vincent's Hospital. He was in a coma from which he never recovered.

Dylan remained in a coma for more than four days. Doctors did whatever could be done, but to no effect. A telegram was sent to Caitlin and she hurried from Laugharne to New York, arriving in a state of great distress. On November 9th, Dylan Thomas died.

There have been many suggestions as to what precisely caused his death: 'Insult to the brain', alcoholic poisoning, diabetic shock, suicide, the effect of the drugs combined with alcohol, pneumonia. Nobody will ever know why this great poet, who had survived with apparent failure for so many years, was unable to live with what was now apparent success.

But then, how can we ever know why this man should have been so ill-equipped in many ways, and yet at the same time be an exceptional writer who illuminated our lives with his vision? Whereas we may be dazzled by waves and reflections on the surface of life, Dylan could see through 'faded eyes to the roots of the sea'.

Caitlin brought his body back to Laugharne where it was buried in the churchyard.

*The grave of
Dylan Thomas,
Laugharne*

Conclusion

Fields of praise

In many ways Dylan appears to have been his own worst enemy: his fears and uncertainty led him into inappropriate behaviour that in the end served only to increase the fear and uncertainty that gave rise to it. The vicious circle led him to an early death in a foreign land.

The tragedy is that, to an outsider, it seems so simple to have stepped off this vicious circle. Dylan was, after all, a great artist. He had, after all, a ferociously devoted and supportive wife. He earned enormous sums of money. He was also a man who could make others want to read poetry, who could hold an audience of a thousand people spellbound with his readings. He was a man of wit, of humour and of endless charm.

He was also frightened of failure and was plagued by fears that he had nothing more to say. He was given to petty theft and to deceit. He was irresponsible, forgetful of his duties as a husband and a father, and often abused the kindness of his friends.

The Dylan Thomas Centre, Swansea

3

Nobody knows who the 'real' Dylan Thomas was: how could they? He never knew himself.

He was a writer of obscure and difficult poems that some of the most cultured minds of our time consider to be great poetry.

So many different people see so many different things in his life and his work that they are perhaps less a glass through which we see another world than a mirror through which we see what we want him to be, what we are ourselves.

Dylan Thomas was a man of Swansea, of Welsh-speaking parents, who left for London and New York, but who never left Wales. Towards the end of his life he found peace in Laugharne, the world within a world.

With the passage of time, the arguments and the scandal about his life will die away, yet his writings will live on, and Dylan Thomas will become the man that his closest and most loyal friend, Vernon Watkins, described: 'the serious survivor of all his myths.'

Acknowledgements

I am greatly indebted to the many friends, biographers, editors and critics who have written about Dylan Thomas. In particular, the works of John Ackerman, John Malcolm Brinnin, Professor Walford Davies, Paul Ferris, Constantine Fitzgibbon, Professor Ralph Maud, Caitlin Thomas, Jeff Towns, George Tremlett, Gwen Watkins, and Vernon Watkins have been invaluable and a reader may look to them for more detailed study than this book is intended to provide.

I am grateful to those who have provided visual material for this book, including Colin James and Mary Johnson and The Carmarthenshire County Council Marketing Photo Library, Ms Susan Beckley and Mr Kim Collis and the Swansea City and County Council Archives and Libraries Division, Phil Alder and Lorraine Scourfield and the Cultural Services Department of Carmarthenshire County Council, Siân Newton of the Photographic Library of the Wales Tourist Board, Swansea City and County Council Economic Development Division and Simon Cobley and the Archive Department of Orion Publishing. I am grateful also to those who have allowed the use of original material in this book, including Mrs Gwen Watkins, David Higham Associates, Orion Publishing, Cwmni Siriol/S4C and the Trustees of the Estate of Dylan Thomas.

A particular debt is owed to Jeff Towns of Dylan's Bookstore, Salubrious Passage, Swansea, whose vast knowledge and no less vast collection of Dylan memorabilia, joined with his unfailing courtesy, has been of immense value. A selection of items from the Jeff Towns/Dylan's Bookstore Collection is displayed at the Dylan Thomas Centre, Swansea.

Bibliography

Dylan Thomas, *Collected Poems 1934 - 1953*,
  edited by Walford Davies and Ralph Maud, Dent, 1988.
Dylan Thomas, *The Collected Stories*, Phoenix, 1992.
Dylan Thomas, *Under Milkwood*, Dent, 1962.

John Ackermann, *Welsh Dylan*, John Jones, 1979.
John Malcolm Brinnin, *Dylan Thomas in America*, Dent, 1956
Paul Ferris, *Dylan Thomas: a biography*,
  Hodder & Stoughton, 1977.
Constantine Fitzgibbon, *The Life of Dylan Thomas*, Dent, 1965.
George Tremlett, *Dylan Thomas: In the mercy of his means*,
  Constable, 1991.
Gwen Watkins, *Portrait of a Friend*, Gomer Press, 1983.

Illustrations

Carmarthenshire County Council Cultural Services: p. 27.
Carmarthenshire County Council Tourism and Marketing
Department: pp. 42, 54, 56, 57, 58, 59, 63, 72. City and County
of Swansea Economic Development Department: pp. 9, 25, 31,
64, 77. City and County of Swansea Archives Department: pp.
16, 18(iii), 23, 24, 29, 41, 47, 49, 62, 75. Orion Publishing &
Jeff Towns/Dylan's Bookstore Collection: pp. 66, 67.
Jeff Towns/Dylan's Bookstore Collection: pp. 4, 10, 15(i), 15(ii),
39, 60. Gweithdy'r Gair: 18(i), 18(ii). Llyfrgell Genedlaethol
Cymru/National Library of Wales: p. 32. Cwmni Siriol/S4C:
pp. 68, 69.